Sasquatch

SASQUATCH

Wild Man of North America

Elaine Landau

The Millbrook Press ❏ Brookfield, Connecticut
Mysteries of Science

Library of Congress Cataloging-in-Publication Data

Landau, Elaine.
Sasquatch, wild man of the woods / by Elaine Landau.
p.   cm.—(Mysteries of Science)
Includes bibliographical references (p.   ) and index.
Summary: Introduces the unidentified apelike Sasquatch said to
dwell in the Pacific Northwest, recounts sightings throughout history,
and discusses the evidence and theories advanced about its existence.
ISBN 1-56294-348-0 (lib. bdg.)
1. Sasquatch—Juvenile literature.   [1. Sasquatch.   2. Monsters.]
I. Title.   II. Series: Landau, Elaine. Mysteries.
QL89.2.S2L36   1993
001.9′44—dc20   92-35144   CIP   AC

Published by The Millbrook Press
2 Old New Milford Road, Brookfield, Connecticut 06804

For Grace Noyes McLaughry

Cover illustration and design, and illustration
on p. 8 by Anne Canevari Green

Photos courtesy of Rene Dahinden: pp. 10, 15,
17, 20, 26, 33, 41; British Columbia Archives
and Records Service: pp. 11, 13; International
Society of Cryptozoology: p. 23; from *The
Province*, October 6, 1958: p. 28; AP/Wide
World Photos: pp. 30, 31; UPI/Bettmann:
p. 36; Photo Researchers: pp. 38 (Tom
McHugh), 40 (Anthony Mercieca).

Contents

ANNE CANEVARI GREEN

Wild Man of the Woods

For years people have told stories of big, hairy, humanlike creatures dwelling in the forests of northern California, Oregon, Washington, and Canada's British Columbia. Standing over 8 feet (244 centimeters) tall, the creatures have been described as having faces like apes, broad shoulders, and long arms. Their coneshaped heads seem to sit directly on their hunched backs due to their short, stout necks.

*In this cartoon an unfortunate fisherman
meets the mysterious Sasquatch—who snacks on his catch.*

These supposed giants of North America have been known by many names. The Indians of southwest British Columbia called the creature Sasquatch, which means "wild man of the woods." By the 1950s the American press had named it Bigfoot because of the oversized tracks it was thought to leave.

Is Sasquatch real or the subject of a centuries-old folktale that has turned into a modern legend?

Jacko and the Hypnotists ❑ There have been hundreds of accounts of encounters with the creature. In July 1884, the *Daily Colonist,* a Victoria, British Columbia, newspaper, ran a headline story describing the supposed capture of a Sasquatch in an area near the Fraser River.

Jacko, as the creature was called, was described as resembling a small gorilla. The newspaper stated that Jacko was 4 feet 7 inches tall (140 centimeters), weighed 127 pounds (58 kilograms), and had a body like a man's—except that it was covered with dark, shiny hair. No one knows for certain what became of Jacko. It was rumored that he eventually wound up in the Barnum and Bailey circus.

WHAT IS IT?

—

**A STRANGE CREATURE CAP-
TURED ABOVE YALE.**

—

A British Columbia Gorilla.

—

(Correspondence of The Colonist).

YALE, B. C., July 3rd, 1882.

In the immediate vicinity of No. 4 tunnel, situated some twenty miles above this village, are bluffs of rock which have hitherto been unsurmountable, but on Monday morning last were successfully scaled by Mr. Onderdonk's employes on the regular train from Lytton. Assisted by Mr. Costerton, the British Columbia Express Company's messenger, and a number of

The Daily Colonist *ran this headline when it reported Jacko's "capture."*

Some think the *Daily Colonist* may have made up the Jacko story to boost sales. Moreover, Jacko could have been an adult chimpanzee or a young gorilla. These animals live in the African tropics, not in the cool climates of the U.S. Pacific Northwest or Canada. But such an animal could have escaped from a traveling circus or carnival show, though none are known to have been in the area at the time.

❏ ❏ ❏

In the early 1900s the number of Sasquatch sightings in the same Fraser River region of British Columbia increased. Yet many people found these stories—often reported in the U.S. and Canadian press—exaggerated and difficult to accept. According to the *Seattle Times* of July 16, 1918, a band of Sasquatches attacked the shack of a man searching for gold near Kelso, Washington. The article described the Sasquatches as creatures that were half human and half monster. Witnesses claimed that they stood over 8 feet (244 centimeters) tall and had the power to both hypnotize humans as well as disappear at will. Even if the story was based on a few facts, it was still barely believable.

Visit with a Sasquatch Family ❏ In 1957 a retired lumberman named Albert Ostman reported one of the most detailed and vivid Sasquatch encounters. In 1924, Ostman was searching for gold at Toba Inlet across from Vancouver Island in British Columbia. Ostman traveled through the area for a week. He

*The Fraser River region, the site of many
reported Sasquatch sightings.*

brought along cooking and eating utensils and the necessary camping equipment. He settled on a campsite among some cypress trees near a cool freshwater stream.

Ostman claimed that on his second night at the camp he woke to find that someone or something was dragging his sleeping bag along the ground—with him in it. He was pulled across rocky terrain for about 25 miles (40 kilometers). Then, suddenly, he felt the sleeping bag being lifted until his body slipped out.

The lumberman found himself surrounded by four Sasquatches—an 8-foot (244 centimeter) father, who captured him, a 7-foot (213 centimeter) mother, and a young son and daughter. According to Ostman, they looked very much like hairy humans but had padded feet with oversized big toes. The Sasquatch family did not threaten or harm their frightened guest. Instead they seemed fascinated by his equipment.

Six days later Ostman was finally able to escape from the creatures and return home. For the next 33 years he never told anyone his story because he thought others would think it was a prank. But on August 20, 1957, Ostman swore before a justice of the peace in Fort Langley, British Columbia, that his statements were true. People who knew him well testified that Ostman was an honest and responsible individual.

Sasquatch Attack ❏ Another of the most famous Sasquatch incidents also supposedly took place in 1924 at a mining camp high in the mountains of Washington State. While a group of

*Many years passed before Albert Ostman (right) agreed
to go public with the story of his Sasquatch encounter.
Here he talks to Sasquatch expert René Dahinden.*

miners were working, one member claimed he saw a frightening, hairy creature approaching from behind some trees. The miner fired his rifle at the animal, who quickly fled into the forest.

Meanwhile, a second miner reportedly fired several times at another creature he spotted on a nearby cliff. Although this miner was certain he had hit the Sasquatch three times and that the animal fell from the cliff into the valley below, no remains were ever recovered.

According to the miners, the Sasquatches took revenge for the shootings during the night, attacking their cabin. The Sasquatches supposedly hurled rocks at the cabin and hit the walls and roof with heavy boards. The assault continued for five hours until the creatures retreated just before dawn. The terrified miners left the next day and never returned.

Of course, the miners could not be certain that they were attacked by Sasquatches. Since their cabin was windowless and no one dared open the door, it was impossible to tell what had caused all the noise outside.

Sasquatch or Bear? ❏ A much publicized Sasquatch encounter known as the Ruby Creek Incident was said to have occurred in September 1941. According to this story, an 8-foot-tall (244 centimeter) male Sasquatch left the woods and wandered onto a remote farm belonging to the Chapman family in British Columbia.

At first Mrs. Chapman, who was home alone with her children, thought she saw a very large bear. But when she

The Chapman house at Ruby Creek,
abandoned at the time of this photo.

realized that she did not know what was on her property, she took her youngsters and ran from the farm.

After several hours Mrs. Chapman returned with her husband and others to find the creature gone. But it had left its mark. There were huge **footprints** in the dirt surrounding the farmhouse and yard. A large barrel of salted fish in a shed near the home had been tipped over, and the fish were scattered about. The Chapmans concluded that whatever had visited their farm that day did not like the taste of salted fish.

William Roe, a British Columbian hunter and woodsman, reported seeing a Sasquatch while hunting in October 1955. Roe, like Mrs. Chapman, thought he glimpsed the biggest grizzly bear he had ever seen. But as he crept closer, Roe realized that it was not a bear at all. Instead there stood a creature about 6 feet 3 inches (191 centimeters) tall with broad shoulders and long, dangling arms. Dark brown hairs with silver tips covered its body. The creature's head seemed larger at the back than in the front. It had a flat nose, wide lips, and ears that looked human. After a few moments, the apelike creature darted off into the woods, and Roe lost sight of him.

❏ ❏ ❏

These are just a few of the hundreds of Sasquatch incidents reported in the Pacific Northwest of the United States and Canada. Many of the reported Sasquatch sightings have been remarkably similar. All of the Sasquatches spotted have walked upright with a slow, shuffling motion. Most have had reddish brown hair, although some have had hair described as black, beige, or silver-tipped. The creatures have usually been muscular and powerfully built.

Although they have been seen throughout the year, the most common months for sightings have been July and August as well as October and November.

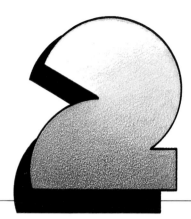

Come Out, Come Out Wherever You Are

A flurry of Sasquatch sightings occurred in the late 1960s and early 1970s. No one knows why sightings were more frequent during this period. Was it possible that the Sasquatch population had increased so that there were more of them to see? Or had the growing popularity of winter sports during this time brought more people into formerly unpopulated areas, perhaps increasing the likelihood of sightings? As Sasquatch sightings became more highly publicized, were people more likely to mistake animals they normally saw in the woods for the creature?

Sasquatch's popularity grew during the late 1960s. René Dahinden poses next to a Sasquatch statue in Willow Creek, California.

Whatever the reasons, many people reported seeing humanlike monsters in the Pacific Northwest as well as in every other state except Rhode Island and Hawaii.

One sighting involved six young men hunting near Freemont, Washington, in November 1966. The hunters thought they saw a large buck in a nearby clearing. But they soon realized that they had come across an immense, two-legged animal. They described the animal as having a massive body covered with short, dark hair. The creature eyed them curiously but did not try to attack the hunters.

Hansen's Carnival Exhibit ❏ In 1970 a man named Frank D. Hansen told of how he shot a Sasquatch in a Minnesota forest. The tale, published in 1970 in *Saga* magazine, described how Hansen had been out hunting with some army friends when he shot and wounded a deer. Hansen tracked the wounded animal as it headed toward a swamp.

When Hansen arrived at the swamp, he reportedly found three Sasquatches finishing the kill and eating the animal raw. When one of the Sasquatches noticed Hansen, it lunged at him. Hansen fired at the creature, killing it instantly. Then he ran back until he reached the others in his hunting party. Hansen, however, said nothing of the incident to his companions, fearing they would laugh at his story.

Hansen claimed he returned to the same swamp weeks later. He reported nearly tripping over the slain Sasquatch's body, which now lay frozen on the snowy ground. Hansen returned home with the body. He kept the creature on ice in a large freezer.

Years later he exhibited the corpse—frozen in a block of ice—in a traveling carnival show. For just over a quarter, people could catch a glimpse of what they were told were a Sasquatch's remains.

But others doubted what was on display. Scientists thought that rather than a Sasquatch corpse, Hansen was exhibiting a human-made monster. The body was an almost comical combination of human and ape. Some suggested that freezing the specimen in an ice block was a brilliant—and underhanded—idea. The exhibit's frosty appearance added an air of mystery while preventing close inspection. In addition, as the frozen Sasquatch's publicity soared, several companies came forward claiming that they had created the ice-covered model for Hansen out of latex rubber.

In response, Hansen stated that the Sasquatch on display was a model. The original, he said, had been carefully hidden away at a secret location. But there was never any scientific evidence that Hansen's original—if one ever existed—was genuine.

No Scientific Evidence ❏ No one has ever captured a live Sasquatch or come across a genuine Sasquatch corpse or skeleton. Scientists have never been able to study a Sasquatch bone

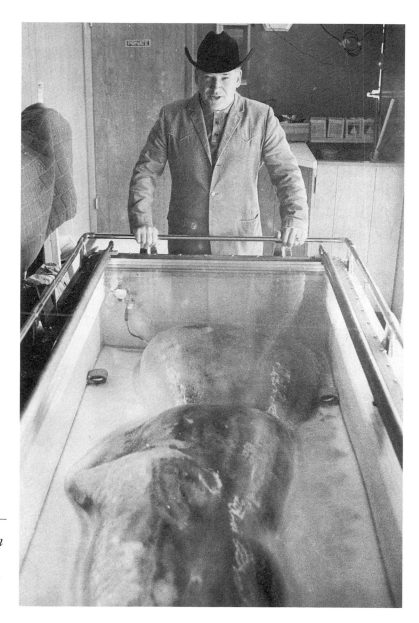

Frank Hansen
stands over
his "monster"
on ice.

or **fossil.** Some Sasquatch trackers have found unusual fecal matter (waste products) and hairs that they could not identify. Museum and university scientists could not reach any positive conclusions about their origins, but some researchers agreed that both the droppings and hair looked very much like a bear's.

Lack of interest in Sasquatch among scientists left Sasquatch scouting to self-appointed monster hunters. At times, individuals who searched for Sasquatch argued that the scientific community purposefully tried to ignore the creature. They stressed that proof of the creature's existence would challenge theories long held by the world's scientists.

Yet museums and university **anthropology** and **zoology** departments felt that the reverse was true. They stated that the discovery of a formerly unknown **primate**—as Sasquatch is thought to be—would usher in an exciting new research era. There is even a branch of science called **cryptozoology** that specializes in studying animals previously unknown or believed extinct. With hard evidence of Sasquatch's existence, hunting expeditions would be organized as cryptozoologists received increased funding to learn more about the mammal. But before this could occur, they would need actual proof that Sasquatch was an animal rather than a myth.

Where's the Proof?

Perhaps the most solid evidence suggesting Sasquatch's existence is the footprints thought to belong to it. Here is the reason why: Humans walk differently than other primates. When people walk, the heel of each foot touches the ground first. Then the body weight shifts to the ball at the front of the foot as the heel is lifted off the ground. Because of this the human foot leaves a distinct print.

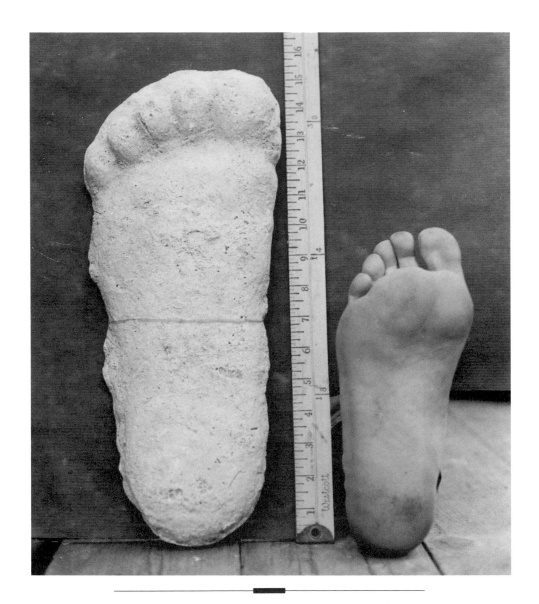

This supposed Sasquatch print (left) is almost one and a half times longer than a human foot.

If Sasquatch were some type of humanlike ape, as many say it is, its footprints would be decidedly different from a human's or other primate's. Sasquatch's toes would be larger than human toes. They would bend more as the creature walked, leaving a deeper print. The first Sasquatch prints, found in mud and river **silt,** show these unusual features, as do later tracks seen in snow.

First Footprints Found? ❑ In 1811 explorer and tracker David Thompson made one of the first reports of these unusual footprints. While crossing the Canadian Rocky Mountains, Thompson discovered a footprint measuring 14 inches (36 centimeters) long and 8 inches (20 centimeters) wide. The print showed four claw marks and a well-developed heel.

Had Thompson seen a large bear's footprint, or did it belong to some unknown creature? Some say it could not have been a bear print because a bear has five toes, while Thompson only saw four. Others point out that a bear's small inner toe might not appear in a print made in mud or snow.

In 1958 a similar discovery was made in northern California. While bulldozing logs in a densely wooded region, a worker named Jerry Crew came across some unusual tracks in the mud. They looked like human footprints except for their large size. The prints measured 16 inches (41 centimeters) long and 7 inches (18 centimeters) wide. The tracks were also quite deep, indicating that whoever or whatever made them weighed a great deal.

*Jerry Crew
with a
cast of
one of the
Sasquatch
prints he
reported
finding.*

When Crew and his work team bulldozed the area again weeks later, they saw similar tracks all around the first ones. Because of the prints' unusual size, Crew made a plaster cast of one of them. A photograph showing him holding the cast appeared in the local newspapers. The footprint reached from his neck to his waist.

Fake Footprints ❏ Hundreds of supposed Sasquatch prints have been uncovered in addition to those found by David Thompson and Jerry Crew. Some of these prints have varied widely in size. Some say these differing footprints suggest that two **species,** or types, of Sasquatch may exist. Scientists believe it extremely unlikely that two types of Sasquatch would exist, if any exist at all. They have proposed that some if not all kinds of prints are not real.

Some alleged Sasquatch footprints are known to be fake. A television producer researching a program on Sasquatch interviewed a road worker named Ron Pickens who described how in 1968 he had created several Sasquatch prints in the Bossburg area of Washington. Pickens said that he nailed a pair of 16-inch-long (41 centimeter) feet he had carved out of wood to his boots. He also claimed he fashioned additional pairs for other family members in varying sizes. Pickens and his family went out walking in the boots, creating strange tracks.

❏ ❏ ❏

In 1982 this man, Rant Mullens, claimed Sasquatch prints he whittled out of wood were used to make tracks in several Sasquatch hoaxes.

Despite these arguments, Sasquatch believers feel that at least some of the footprints may be real. Sasquatch tracks have been found over large portions of rugged mountain **terrain.** In some of these regions it would be difficult for any human to travel while operating a print-making device or wearing cumbersome boots with footprint attachments. At times the prints have trailed off into especially rocky, difficult-to-reach spots.

Some people feel these and other steep, heavily wooded spots could be home to a number of large primates.

Perhaps one of the most exciting Sasquatch discoveries occurred in 1982 when a Forest Service patrolman uncovered some new footprints near Walla Walla, Washington. The patrolman made a plaster cast of the prints, which were 15 inches (38 centimeters) long and contained tiny lines on the soles. Such lines are found only on human feet and those of higher ape forms.

Several fingerprint experts identified the prints as genuine. Even when presented with a fake version, they were not fooled. Researchers have continued studying these prints to learn more about the animal that made them.

Washington State University scientist Grover Krantz holds up a cast of one of the Walla Walla prints. The prints, he said, convinced him that Sasquatch was real.

Yet scientists pointed out that in determining if Sasquatch is real, other data besides prints must also be considered. Scientists frequently examine fossils to study the past. But while fossil remains of early humans have been recovered, none belonging to large apes has ever been found in the area where Sasquatches have been reportedly seen.

Sasquatch on Film? ❏ Some Sasquatch hunters have tried to present photographic evidence of their findings. But scientists doubt that these hunters' photos and movie footage of the creature are real.

Perhaps the Sasquatch film that received the most attention was shot in 1967 by a man named Roger Patterson. Patterson worked in a rodeo and had been involved in show business. He developed an interest in Sasquatch and set out to find the creature.

In the fall of 1967, Patterson and a friend combed Bluff Creek Valley in northern California where there had been many Sasquatch sightings. According to Patterson, the two men found a female Sasquatch. Patterson's horse threw him when the creature appeared, and he pursued the Sasquatch on foot. He tried to keep his camera focused on the female Sasquatch as he ran after her.

Roger Patterson's famous photo of what he claimed was a female Sasquatch.

The Mystery Continues

As the Sasquatch mystery continues, many wonder: Is Sasquatch just a myth? Some Sasquatch hunters have spent years trying to prove otherwise. They point to the fact that hundreds of people in both the United States and Canada claim to have either seen these creatures or their footprints. Since most of these people do not know one another and have nothing to gain from lying, there is little reason to doubt their truthfulness.

Explorer C. Thomas Biscardi searched for Sasquatch for ten years before snapping this picture of what he says is the creature in 1981.

Even if some of these people were trying to fool the public, it is unlikely that all would be. Some of those involved in Sasquatch encounters or sightings are known as responsible community members. They have included sheriffs, forest rangers, company supervisors, and state police officers. Sasquatch is even regarded as an endangered species in one Washington county and protected by law. Anyone who kills or harms one may be fined up to $5,000 or spend up to one year in the county jail.

Sasquatch investigators also stress that many more people may have sighted these creatures than is known. People who have reported seeing a Sasquatch have been ridiculed by their families, friends, and neighbors. Some have insisted on not having their identities made public. Because of this others may feel too embarrassed to tell anyone what they have seen.

Nevertheless, it is still difficult for many people to imagine apelike creatures over 8 feet (244 centimeters) tall and weighing more than 700 pounds (318 kilograms) living in remote forests. Where would they have come from?

Sasquatch Origins ❏ Some Sasquatch hunters think that the creature may be related to the **Neanderthals**—humans of early times. Although the exact date is not known, it is generally thought these humans populated the Americas beginning about 125,000 years ago. Is it possible that these people **migrated** from Asia to Alaska across a wide plain connecting the regions and traveled south? At that time the Americas' abundant game would have attracted these early hunters.

In this depiction a Neanderthal man builds a fire.

Since Neanderthals had already lived in a cold climate, they could easily have adapted to the lower temperatures of the Northwest.

Scientists, however, feel it is highly unlikely that Sasquatches descended from these Neanderthals. Neanderthals were distinctly more "human" than the Sasquatches sighted. They would have been further advanced at the time of their migration than Sasquatches as they have been described.

These early people were also able hunters who fashioned their own weapons and cooking utensils out of stone. They also learned to use fire for warmth and to cook their food. Neanderthals maintained elaborate burial ceremonies for their dead. Although Sasquatches may leave footprints similar to those of humans, no evidence has suggested that these creatures used tools or fire or had developed their culture.

Some Sasquatch believers have suggested that the creature may instead be related to an even earlier, more primitive people than the Neanderthals. Perhaps these people could also have migrated from Asia to America. However, there is no proof of this theory. And other people insist that since Sasquatches spotted in North America are distinctly more like apes than humans, they could not have evolved from such **prehistoric** people.

Other Questions and Theories ❏ Other questions about Sasquatch abound. How could they survive the cold snowy winters when fruits, berries, and other forest foods are scarce? One theory is that Sasquatches eat excessively through the summer and **hibernate** during the winter. While they remain dormant, their bodies exist on the extra fat they have acquired during the warm months.

However, this theory does not match the information gathered from sightings. Although there have been fewer winter sightings, Sasquatches have been seen during every month of the year. In addition, if such creatures hibernated they would appear fat just prior to winter. But they have not been described that way in late autumn encounters.

Some say if Sasquatch exists it may be related to the lowland gorilla, pictured (left) with its baby. Does this totem (right)— belonging to a tribe of Native Americans in what is now Canada— depict lowland gorillas living in North America's woods?

Another theory holds that during the colder months, Sasquatches migrate, or travel, toward the seacoast as some other animals do. There they would exist largely on fish and other seafood until spring. A third theory is that Sasquatches get food during the warm months and store it during winter. The cold would serve as a natural freezer, allowing the primates to use it as needed throughout the winter. That might explain Sasquatch tracks seen by skiers at unusually high elevations where it is very cold.

Despite these theories, most scientists argue that it would be nearly impossible for an unknown primate to thrive in northern America's cool forest regions.

Still, many people insist that something lurks in the woods—something that leaves nearly human footprints, something that remains a mystery.

Glossary

anthropology—study of the physical, social, and cultural development of humans.

cryptozoology—branch of science that specializes in the study of animals previously unknown or believed extinct.

evolution—process by which a species of plant or animal changes its defining characteristics slowly over millions of years.

footprint—mark or impression left on a surface by a foot.

fossil—impression of an animal or plant from an earlier age preserved in rock.

hibernate—to pass the winter in an inactive, sleeplike state.

migrate—to move from one area to a new area, usually for improved living conditions.

Neanderthal—type of early human that lived over 40,000 years ago.

prehistoric—describing the era before written history.

primates—specific animals, including monkeys, apes, and humans, that are believed to have a common ancestor.

silt—loose layer of soil usually made up of small particles of rock.

species—biological term meaning a classification of related plants or animals capable of breeding with one another.

terrain—land area.

zoology—branch of biology concerned with the study of animals.

Further Reading

Arnold, Caroline. *Trapped in Tar: Fossils From the Ice Age.* New York: Clarion Books, 1987.

Asimov, Isaac. *How Did We Find Out About Our Human Roots?* New York: Walker & Co., 1979.

Carmichael, Carrie. *Bigfoot: Man, Monster or Myth?* Milwaukee, Wisconsin: Raintree Publications, 1977.

Christian, Mary B. *Bigfoot.* New York: Crestwood House, 1986.

Cole, Joanna. *Evolution.* New York: Crowell, 1987.

Cole, Joanna. *The Human Body: How We Evolved.* New York: William Morrow 1987.

Lerner, Carol. *A Forest Year.* New York: William Morrow, 1987.

Matthews, Rupert. *Ice Age Animals.* New York: Bookwright Press, 1990.

Parsons, Alexandra. *Amazing Mammals.* New York: Alfred A. Knopf, 1990.

Riha, Susanne. *Animals in Winter.* New York: Carolrhoda Books, 1989.

Index

About the Author

Elaine Landau received her Bachelor's degree
from New York University in English and
Journalism and her Master's degree in Library
and Information Science from Pratt Institute.
She has worked as a newspaper reporter, editor,
and youth services librarian, and has especially
enjoyed writing over 55 books for young people.

Although Ms. Landau and her small white dog Max
have searched the woods for unknown creatures,
they have only seen deer.